The Beautiful Butterfly

Marcello Pennacchio

Copyright © 2022
Marcello Pennacchio
All rights reserved
ISBN- 978-1-922727-34-3

Linellen Press
265 Boomerang Road
Oldbury WA 6121
www.linellenpress.com.au

Dedication

Dedicated to all the lost butterflies out there, especially Brenda, Diodato and Michael!

Somewhere on a leaf,
a teeny-weeny caterpillar
crawls out of her egg!

What will she do with herself?

She will eat many leaves and grow.

Her stripes will tell the little birdie to leave her alone.

into a beautiful butterfly.

She will fly for days and days, travelling long distances!

She will love flowers and they will love her!

She will find a mate and start a family.

She will lay tiny eggs on leaves. They are as small as a grain of sand.

She will bring hope to those who need it.

Then, one day, her work will all be done and there is nothing left for her to do. She will feel sad!

Goodbye butterfly!

Wait! The beautiful butterfly lives on in her young. Hello butterflies!

The Marvellous Migrating Monarch

The monarch butterly is one of the most recognisable insects on the planet. Originally from North America, this migrating marvel has since colonised other parts of the world, including the Pacific and Australia.

In the Americas, where it is indigenous, the caterpillar's main source of food is the milkweed plant, which produces powerful heart poisons that can kill its predators without harming itself. The caterpillar's stripes serve as a warning to its would-be eaters that they are poisonous.

The life cycle of the monarch is comprised of five distinct stages (right). Once the caterpillar has grown, it undergoes one of the truly magnificent processes in life – metamorphosis. One of the main advantages of such a dramatic change, which can take from 8 – 15 days, is it eliminates competition for food between the juvenile and adult forms of this species. It also gives it access to more varieties of food.

Sadly, monarch butterfly numbers are dwindling, with conservation efforts all around the world desperately trying to save them from further decline. We can all do our part to save them by conserving the plants they eat and preserving the habitats they occupy.

For more information, go to: **https://www.worldwildlife.org/species/monach-butterfly**

Here are some other fun facts:

- Scientific name: *Danaus plexippus.* It means "sleepy transformation!" in Greek.
- As the caterpillar emerges, it eats its own egg shell.
- They fly via a slow-motion clapping of their wings.
- Migrating monarchs can fly thousands of kilometres each year!
- Monarchs have been bred on the International Space Station.
- In North America, the viceroy butterfly is almost identical to the monarch and is often confused for it. This form of mimicry (copying) confuses its predators.

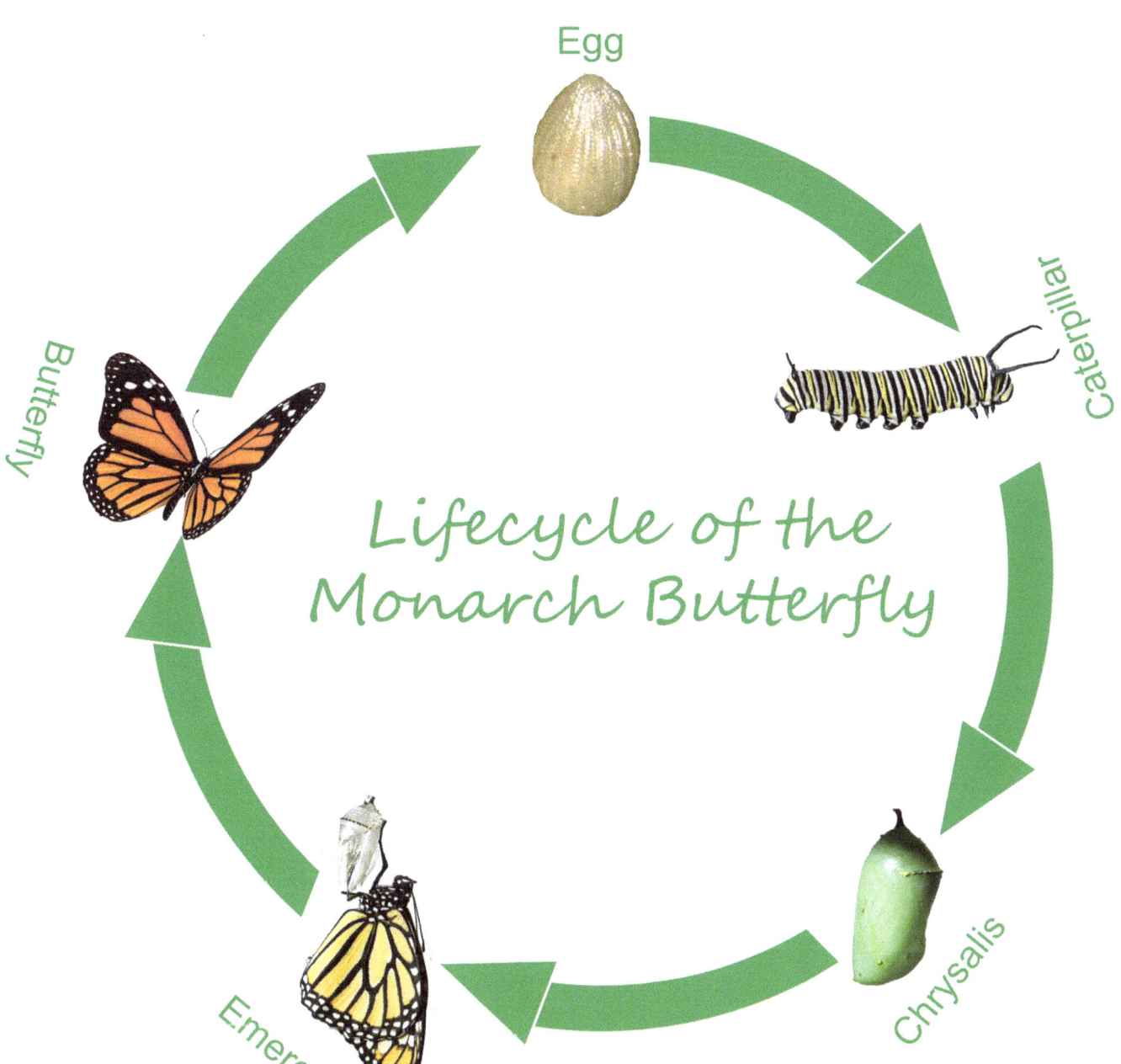

About the author:

For over 30 years, I have been a scientist, a teacher and a writer. As a scientist, I have discovered new heart medicines from plants used by the Amazing Australian Aboriginal People, I have identified plants that produce chemicals that both inhibit and promote the germination and growth of other plants and I have found a disease that turns lizard blood green. As a teacher, I have taught English, Science, HASS and Mathematics to primary and secondary school students in Australia, as well as Biology and Ethnobotany to tertiary students in Australia and the United States. Finally, as a writer, I have written children's books for Scholastic Australia and Linellen Press, and reference books for Oxford University Press. Nothing gives me greater joy than to educate people.

Other children's books by this author:

1. Somewhere in Australia (Scholastic)
2. Somewhere in the reef (Scholastic)
3. Our Backyard Zoo (Linellen)

Illustrations

With a few exceptions, all the illustrations in this book were prepared by the author using his own photographs and rendered using the freely available online software, FotoSketcher 3.70 (fotosketcher.com). A donation was made to the developer of this excellent software. Seven photographs were purchased from Shutterstock: 103565036, 3427934, 491116675, 2436097, 1649042476, 1164172324 and 739338931 (Shutterstock.com).

The front cover was painted by the late, Brenda Doreen Jefferson, and was used here with the permission of her husband, Roger Jefferson.

Marcello Pennacchio BSc (Hons), PhD, Dip.Ed.

www.ingramcontent.com/pod-product-compliance
Lightning Source LLC
Chambersburg PA
CBHW051250110526
44588CB00025B/2941